Maya 2012 Revealed

Demystifying the Prophecy

Jeanine Kitchel

Cover design by Nicholas Kitchel
E-book formatting by Sun Editing & Book Design

First edition

Kitchel, Jeanine Lee
Maya 2012 Revealed, Demystifying the Prophecy/
Jeanine Kitchel

Includes bibliographical references
ISBN: 978-0-615-66017-2-(soft cover)
ISBN: 978-0-615-58567-3 (e-book)

Printed and bound in the USA

Acknowledgments

As always, my sincere thanks to the gracious people of Maya Mexico, in Quintana Roo, Yucatan and Chiapas.

"What do the Maya and Albert Einstein
have in common? Both sought harmony by trying
to combine space with time."
—Anthony Aveni, Archaeo-astronomer

Contents

Introduction   7

1   Who Are the Maya   9

2   Breaking the Code   16

3   The Calendars   26

4   Gone Viral: Maya Stellae and the 2012 Debate   35

5   2012ologists: Who, What, Why?   44

6   The Milky Way and the Precession of the Equinoxes   53

7   Collapse of the Maya   58

8   Prophecy   64

Bibliography

Introduction

Several catch phrases have gone mainstream in the past few years—Maya prophecy, end date, 2012ologists and December 21, 2012. We've been deluged with information about the day made famous by the notorious Maya calendar.

Who are the Maya and why do they have such a profound impact on our imaginations? Does their calendar predict the world's end December 21, 2012?

To consider the prediction, we have to examine what is known about the Maya. They've been a media sensation since early Yucatan explorers John Lloyd Stephens and artist Frederick Catherwood stumbled onto pyramid site Copán, Honduras, in 1839, and wrote *Incidents of Travel in Central America, Chiapas and Yucatan*. This bestseller propelled not just the Maya to fame but both Stephens and Catherwood, too. Today, nearly two centuries later, the Maya are still making headlines. Why the fuss?

The Maya civilization is known to be the greatest of all new world cultures and the only fully literate society in Mesoamerica. But in the ninth century they abandoned the northern sites in the Yucatan and deserted their temples in the central lowlands. Maya cities disappeared, lost in forest jungles, all but forgotten until Stephens and Catherwood's discovery. This mystery has never stopped intriguing us. That's part of the draw. Why did they leave? Where did they go? And what did they know about our future?

December 21, 2012, brings to an end one of the most important cycles of Maya time, a 5,125-year cycle called the thirteen *baktuns*. Did the Maya believe the world would end with this cycle?

Any book that discusses the 2012 prophecy must consider not only who the Maya are, but also the importance of recent breakthroughs in deciphering the Maya code, for without the ability to read Maya glyphs, there would be no inkling that an "end date" existed. With such an abundance of 2012 doomsday literature on the bookshelves, it's hard to know what to believe and how to piece together the information. Through research, I've gained an overall understanding of their civilization and specifics about the end date prophecy. I share my findings here. Hopefully I've covered all bases—from the earliest history of the Maya, their calendars, their astronomy and their collapse, to the meaning of the end date on the Long Count calendar, December 21, 2012.

Chapter 1

Who Are the Maya?

"These people are gods."
—Bob Rands, archeologist at Pakal's tomb,
Palenque, Mexico.

When I first traveled to Quintana Roo in 1983, the Maya code had yet to be broken. Maya culture remained steeped in mystery. If they left clues about their existence in pyramid temples deep within Central American jungles, no scholars could unravel them. What they posted on cement slabs called Maya stellae—their form of Facebook, on display for everyone to read—was indecipherable, at least for the time being. (Later these glyphs would be acknowledged as important dates of accessions, births, deaths and triumphs of their kings). Until recent breakthroughs, modern archeologists and iconographers could not decipher what information the Maya had streamed to the world. It would take one hundred and fifty years to break the code.

So who were the mysterious Maya? Were they astronomers? Mathematicians? Pyramid builders? Lords of the jungle? High priests and shaman? Like all indigenous American people, the Maya's predecessors were nomadic hunters who followed large game animals across the Bering Land Bridge in three migratory waves. As hunter-gatherers they populated the Yucatan Peninsula and the highlands to the south since 11,000

BC. Although no one knows their exact origins, it's guessed they were related to the Olmecs.

Early signs of Maya history surfaced in 300 BC when kings were assigned a ranking known as *ahau*. At the same time they began carving monuments, or stellae, at the highlands' sites. Public art decorated their temples in the lowlands. Kingships were recorded.

Their civilization has been divided into three stages: pre-classic from 1500 BC to 200 AD, classic from 200 AD to 900 AD when the first great civilization in Mesoamerica was established, and finally post-classic from 900 AD to 1200 AD.

Their rise to power, around 600 AD, lasted four hundred years, the length of a *baktun*, one of their time measurements, in which all major classic sites—Palenque, Copán, Tikal, Quiriguá—were built.

The Maya classic era epitomized the best of civilization. They had organized cities, a complex religious system, an advanced calendar, trade and dynastic leadership.

The Maya never fell under the dominion of one sole king nor forged a singular alliance, however. Their city-states were politically autonomous yet culturally and economically inter-dependent.

They learned to farm three thousand years ago, and the cycle of maize became a metaphor for Maya life. Due to the lay of the land, slopes needed terracing and wet fields in swamps needed to be excavated to create raised fields and canals. Forests were slashed and burned and this method of agriculture is still used in the region today.

In the southern lowlands they had either too much rain—sometimes up to 150 inches a year—or too little. Run-off water went north to the Usumacinta River and its tributaries and the Gulf of Mexico and the rest flowed east to the Caribbean Sea. In the northern Yucatan, where there are virtually no rivers, they built reservoirs and used sinkholes known as *cenotes* for water caches.

Wide roads, or *sac-be*, linked parts of their kingdoms, but they had no known highways. The canoe was their major mode of transport.

The magnificent rain forest was a fact of Maya life: mahogany, *zapote* and the great *ceiba,* their tree of life, flourished here. The tree was another metaphor for the Maya—it represented human power--and kings were depicted on monuments in the guise of a world tree.

They fought their wars in the dry season that ran from January to May.

They used cacao beans, jade, obsidian, red shiny oyster shells, cloth and salt as currency.

The Maya followed the beat of a different drummer: they had no metal yet they created intricate, artistic carvings using stone tools and obsidian instead; they had no animals large enough to carry cargo so humans became their beasts of burden, and still they established extensive trade routes with far-flung partners; they did not have the wheel but "invented" a concept for zero.

They utilized three main calendars—the *tzolkin*, the *haab* and the Long Count calendar (Chapter 3). The Long Count calendar, one of the world's most extraordinary renderings of marking time, seems tied to the rise of Maya civilization. But as ninth century AD came to a close and scores of Maya kingdoms fell, the Long Count calendar faded from use. At the same time, divine kingship declined. The Long Count and sacred rulers shared a common destiny: they rose and died together.

Time was cyclical to the Maya and they marked it in segments. A *katun* was twenty years. A *baktun* was nearly four hundred years (three hundred and ninety four to be exact) and the *tzolkin*, or sacred round calendar, was two hundred and sixty days, roughly the length of human gestation or the time it took to complete a planting cycle of maize. The *haab* calendar lasted three hundred and sixty days, but added five days at the end that was like another year. This was needed to comprise a full sidereal cycle or rotation of the earth around the sun. They were not only aware of the time it took for the earth to revolve around the sun, but they were so precise in their calculations that they computed its accuracy to within one-one thousandth of a decimal point of modern science's calculation.

They viewed time differently than we do. Their calendars constantly repeated; their past always returned in endless cycles and repetitive patterns so they could read their future through their past.

The Maya were naked eye astronomers. They kept track of the age of the moon.

They kept records of eclipse cycles and calendars for synchronization of the cycles of Mercury, Venus, Mars, Jupiter and Saturn. Their precision, without the use of modern technology, was due to their persistence. For hundreds of years, month after month, they religiously recorded the minutia of cosmological events. These meticulous and accurate calculations were based on repetition and volume.

The night sky was of utmost importance to the Maya. They viewed the sky as a crocodilian monster. At sundown, *Xibalba*, the underworld, rotated above the earth and became their night sky.

They believed rain would come when it shed blood in conjunction to sacrifices or royal bloodletting made by their kings and queens on earth below. Considered a divinatory practice, rulers pierced ears, tongues or genitals, allowing the blood to collect on paper in a sacred bowl. Then they burned the papers and sometimes a "vision serpent" would appear, to communicate sacred knowledge.

They had a writing system and wrote and recorded events in paper bark books, creating thousands of these codices. Spanish zealots who feared they supported idol worship burned all but three. The remaining codices concern astronomy and depict lunation records and eclipse cycles and are known by the names of the cities in which they surfaced: Dresden, Madrid and Paris. Though the paper bark books are all but gone, hieroglyphics, texts and scenes saved on Maya buildings, stellae, jade, bone and pottery have withstood the decay of the tropics, along with the unreasonable destruction of all things Maya by the church in the sixteenth century.

At its height, 800 AD, their civilization supported millions of people. Tikal in Guatemala was their largest city ever with a one-time population of 50,000. An average Maya site had a population of 30,000. It's been recorded that as many as fifty independent states encompassed more than 100,000 square miles of forest and plains.

Around 830 AD they deserted their major ceremonial centers--their decline had begun, and then came the abrupt disappearance of the classic Maya. The exact reason for the collapse remains unknown, but speculations abound, ranging from peasant revolts, epidemics, foreign invaders, and drought and over population (Chapter 7). The classic Maya were long gone by the time the Spanish arrived in 1527; they were not a force to be reckoned with.

The First Mesa Redonda of Palenque, Mexico, which

produced the earliest results in cracking the code, was held December 1973. After convening for five years, this group of enlightened archeologists, iconographers and epigraphers--David Freidel, Linda Schele, Peter Mathews, David Kelley, Michael Coe, Floyd Lounsbury, George Stuart and Merle Greene Robertson among others--finally gave Yuro Knorozov, the Russian epigrapher who was incremental in the decipherment, his due.

Because of the advances made by this group of Mayanists, we know that December 21, 2012, was a benchmark day for the Maya because it ended one full precessional cycle of 26,000 years. Even today, however, some scholars question if the Maya were aware of the precession of the equinoxes (Chapter 6).

Thirteen and twenty are the building blocks of Maya time philosophy. Thirteen is important because it equals the number of layers in Maya heaven, and twenty because, like us, the Maya used digits on their body when counting: we count only ten fingers, they count both fingers and toes, equaling twenty.

We know the Maya thrived in a distinguished and sophisticated culture, according to art historian and acclaimed epigrapher Linda Schele, who died in 1998.

"Their art involved a level of graphic imagination and expertise that is unparalleled. When Europe was in the Dark Ages, the Maya city-states reached the height of their glory, supporting hundreds of thousands of people," Schele stated in the documentary **Breaking the Maya Code**.

The last recorded Long Count inscription was 910 AD, six centuries before the Spanish arrived. The Maya abandoned the Long Count of their own volition; the conquistadors did not force it on them.

The Maya are hardly a people of the past as today they're seven million strong, living in Mexico, Guatemala, Belize and Western Honduras, still speaking one of thirty-five Mayan languages in their native tongue.

And lastly, we know December 21, 2012, is the end of their Great Long Count cycle, written as 13.0.0.0.0 or 4 *Ahau* 3 *Kankin*, the day when the thirteen *baktuns* (5,125 years) will end. Some archeologists suggest the Great Long Count cycle will roll over into a new beginning, similar to our Y2K date, as in the changing of a millennium (Chapter 8). What does this date signify?

Chapter 2

Breaking the Code

"Over the past few decades, an adverse group of
epigraphers and historians, ethnographers and
archeologists, astronomers and linguists,
artists and amateurs, have finally unlocked
the secret of the glyphs. Today over ninety
percent of the script is understood."
—From the documentary, *Breaking the Maya Code.*

In my many years as a Mayaphile in Mexico, I made
certain to read each and every book on the Maya I
came across. I began with the old explorers: Sylvanus
Morley, Edward Thompson, John Lloyd Stephens and
artist Frederick Catherwood, August LePlongeon, J. Eric
Thompson. Then I read *The Lost World of Quintana
Roo* by Michel Peissel, *Footloose Scientist in Mayan
America* by Sister Mary Corde Lorage, and *The Last
Lords of Palenque* by Victor Perrera and Robert Bruce.

Often these books read like adventure tales, written for the unschooled Maya lover like myself. From
these sources I gained background on various sites and
from this newly gained knowledge, I tiptoed into the
field. After devouring these long gone archeologists, I
leapfrogged into Michael Coe, David Freidel and Linda
Schele, Dennis and Barbara Tedlock and Jeremy Sabroff

on moving to Mexico. Wonderfully current authors and working archeologists save Schele, an art historian and university professor in Alabama who died in 1998, it was as if hundreds of years had gone by, so different was the tone set by modern Mayanists. I have to say, it was an electrifying time. And I was lucky enough to be there at the source as it all came together, hunkered down in a little bookshop on a rustic town square in a tiny pueblo in southern Mexico.

Pyramids, beaches, the Maya—that's what drew me to Mexico. I had no idea I was just beginning a saga that in a few years' time would encompass buying property, opening a bookstore and getting hooked on this ancient culture. Through a series of incidents that could only be called luck, my husband Paul and I met a man on an early trip who became the impetus for selling our house in California and relocating to a small fishing village in the heart of Maya land, Puerto Morelos.

Puerto Morelos was a perfect jumping off spot for day trips or longer adventures to many famous pyramid sites. We were an hour's drive from Tulum; one and a half hours to Chichen Itza by paid highway; less than two hours to Cobá, which was like the movie *Romancing the Stone,* it was so remote. In Cobá we stayed at the isolated Villas Arqueologicas, oftentimes as the only guests in the hotel. Driving to Palenque in Chiapas took longer but we could make it in ten hours if we packed a lunch and just made a pit stop for gas in Escarcega. Certainly one of the Yucatan's least appealing towns, Escarcega became a tourist stop through sheer necessity: it had the only gas station for two hundred miles. Otherwise we'd have seen it in our rear view mirror.

We always traveled to Palenque once a year just to be stunned by those mystical pyramids and to hear the sound of howler monkeys roaring in the nearby jungle.

Paul said Palenque looked like Hawaii with pyramids and it did. The Chiapas rainforest still got plenty of rain (our climate in the northern Yucatan was changing from tropical rainforest to neo-tropical) and flowering heliconia, ginger, birds of paradise, grew wild everywhere.

Then there was the Puuc Route, just south of Merida, Yucatan, that included the sites of Uxmal, Labna, Sayil and Edzna. It was a four-hour drive at most. Uxmal was the stunner here with a handful of towering pyramids, the jewel in the crown being the Pyramid of the Magician. We loved the Uxmal light show and often stayed in a jungle lodge across the road from the pyramids, walking back to our room in the pitch black night with only the stars to guide us--the same stars the Maya looked at, we reminded ourselves, a thousand years earlier.

By the time we moved to Mexico on a full time basis I was an old hand at studying the Maya. Operating the bookstore ignited my interest and gave me access not only to current books on the subject but to a world of locals, travelers and explorers who were up to date on all the latest events taking place in the archeological world.

Although many Maya topics were debatable, one thing everyone agreed on was this: a mystery concealed what this ancient civilization left abandoned in pyramids and palaces deep in rain forest jungles, often secluded from cities and miles away from major thoroughfares. Modern archeologists couldn't yet decipher what information the Maya left behind, but this ancient civilization had been prolific.

Their stellae, brimming with glyphs, revealed illustrations of lords, scribes, depictions of war-like scenes and religious events. What did they mean? Were they anniversaries or epitaphs? Philosophies or accession dates? One enormous problem remained: no one could read Maya hieroglyphics. The world was awed by the Maya, but stymied.

Fast forward 150 years after Central American explorers Stephens and artist Catherwood stumbled onto their first pyramid site in 1839 and only then did modern researches make headway in "breaking" the code.

~~~~~

In visiting the sites and talking to archeologists who'd pop into the bookstore, I learned in the mid-nineties that a breakthrough was near; archeologists and epigraphers (those who study inscriptions) were fitting the final pieces together. A rumor spread--the code had been broken; this was big news, earth shattering, especially in Quintana Roo. I was excited about the breakthrough and knew it would totally change the way the Maya world was viewed.

Frequently customers would ask what the hieroglyphics stood for. I'd direct them to *The Maya*, by Michael Coe, *A Forest of Kings* by Linda Schele and David Friedel, *The Ancient Maya* by Sylvanus Morley, pretty much the core group of books that would give background basics to anyone interested in the Maya. And me, I would gobble up anything new I could find on Maya culture, hieroglyphics, the sites, the calendar. By this time I was seriously addicted.

I decided to re-read Stephens and Catherwood's book to get an idea of the excitement they felt on finding the pyramids. Right after their first Yucatan journey in the mid 1800s they published the best selling book *Incidents of Travel in Central America, Chiapas and Yucatan*, and from that moment on, ancient Maya writing took on a life of its own in the public imagination.

The detailed illustrations of ruined cities and vine covered temples drawn by Catherwood, still the finest and most accurate ever made of many of the Yucatec sites, accompanied Stephens' written accounts. This assured the book bestseller status and enabled Stephens to quit his day job as an attorney when he returned home to the States, so great was the clamor for the book and the information it held.

Over the years, fascination with the Maya world didn't wane, it escalated.

As decades passed and research dragged on, scholars came to believe these silent monuments held names and deeds of kings and nobles and their personal accounts of how a civilization worked towards prosperity, literally carving out their place in history. But until the late 1970s that history perplexed archeologists and aficionados alike. No one knew the secrets of the Maya.

The list of scholars who worked to break the code is a long one, touching on every dignitary in the Maya hall of fame. Through chance and almost two hundred years of striving, an eccentric nineteenth century naturalist named Constantine Rafinesque became interested in the strange writing from Mexico and started moving the cog in the wheel. He determined it was Mayan. He published reports of various adventurers' travels to Chiapas in *The Saturday Evening Post* in 1827 with the first modern decipherments of the language. He also sent copies to a famous Egyptologist who specialized in deciphering Egyptian hieroglyphics.

But it was Stephens' and Catherwood's book that inspired scholars world wide to take a shot at breaking the code. Ernst Forstemann, a German librarian at the Royal Library in Dresden, first worked out the fundamentals of the Maya calendar and figured out basic questions of reading order by the turn of the twentieth century. Forstemann located a copy of the Dresden codex, one of the three surviving codices of Maya writings, and started tinkering with its elusive contents. He made key observations on the book's numerology and his observations led to the first detailed understanding of the Maya calendar and to the eventual decipherment of Maya hieroglyphics.

Explorer Alfred Maudslay published photographs and sketchings in the late 1800s. His drawings of the inscriptions made study of the Maya glyphs possible. Then a newspaper editor, Joseph Goodman of Virginia City, Nevada, contacted Maudslay and collaborated with him focusing on texts from Copán, Quiriguá, and Palenque. He had a breakthrough and these laypersons were the first to crack the code.

Initially scholars jousted about what the stellae and engravings represented. Some thought the texts recorded history. Then famed archeologist Sylvanus Morley, who had spent twenty years excavating Chichen Itza, and supposedly the prototype for Spielberg and Lucas' Indiana Jones, agreed. But unfortunately Morley's aggressive and most adept student-collaborator, J. Eric Thompson, pooh-poohed the idea in 1951 and insisted that he "conceived the endless progress of time that was the supreme mystery of the Maya religion...and in such a setting there was no place for personal records, for in relation to the vastness of time, man and his doings shrink to insignificance. To add details of war or peace, of marriage or giving in marriage, is as though a tourist were to carve his initials on Donatello's David."

Well, that statement by Thompson lead-pipe cinched what any archeologist worth his bones would believe for many years to come. In the fifties, Thompson was the pre-eminent Maya scholar. No one contradicted his theories. Luckily before he died Thompson admitted he'd been wrong and retracted the statement. This allowed the major achievements made by iconographer Tatiana Proskouriakoff, a Russian aristocrat by birth, to shine. She maintained that texts on stellae were in fact dates of kings, which probably marked births, accession to power and conquests.

It's hard to understand why it took so long for Maya archeologists to recognize what seems so simple now. Proskouriakoff's vision of who the Maya were altered the way we view them today. Without her push, who knows how long it would have taken for the Maya code to be broken?

Though no single researcher ever equaled Proskouriakoff's contributions (she put every single glyph she ever saw at any pyramid site on an index card) in 1958 Heinrich Berlin identified the name of glyphs of historical interest at Palenque and glyphs which referred to Maya cities. But still, epigraphers did not know how the Maya spelled their words.

According to David Freidel, co-author of **A Forest of Kings**, that breakthrough came from Russian Yuri Knorozov in 1952 who proposed the Maya system might be similar to Egyptian hieroglyphics, suggesting it could be a system composed of word signs combined with signs representing the sounds of syllables.

But none of the big three—Proskouirakoff, Thompson or Berlin—would give Knorozov the time of day and agree with his theory that the writing was phoneticism. Part of this was due to the politics of the fifties, the beginning of the Cold War with Russia and the division of lines between east and west. Had Knorozov called Paris or London home, perhaps his comrades across the pond would have blessed his proposals.

It wasn't until the first Mesa Redonda of Palenque in 1973 that unknown Western scholars came aboard for the Maya ride and stood the archeological world on its ear. Enter Michael Coe and Floyd Lounsbury. At that first Palenque conference a new generation of epigraphers was initiated into the Maya mysteries including Linda Schele and Peter Mathews. In part started by Merle Green Robertson, best known for her thousands of Maya inscription rubbings, and Moises Morales, the first tour guide at Palenque and self taught Maya scholar, the conference blended Knorozov's phoneticism with Proskouriakoff's historical approach.

Although Knorozov would never receive credit for his achievement or live to see how right he'd been, during the next five years real strides were made as this group of epigraphers developed a collaborative approach and forged the last key, according to Freidel, that the writing reflected spoken language and had word order that produced glyphs, even though they could not yet be read.

Finally they could decide what a word meant by where it fell in a sentence. This enabled the epigraphers to paraphrase inscriptions and deal with them as whole texts. A breakthrough. Through these combined approaches—phoneticism, the historical approach expounded by Proskouriakoff, and 'syntactical analysis' that Thompson the Great insisted was the right system –it came together.

For over a century explorers from Sylvanus Morley and Edward Thompson to Augustus LePlongeon tried to figure out the stories left on Maya stellae at Uxmal and Chichen Itza.

But it wasn't until an art history professor from Alabama, Linda Schele, came to Palenque and was offered a seat at the round table that it all came together. Even Russian iconographer Tatiana Proskouriakoff didn't have the luck and foresight that Schele had. Since her death in 1998 her fans have heralded her efforts: love of the Maya pyramids and her artist's sensibilities compounded and empowered her to break the Maya code.

The story goes like this. On the last day of the Mesa Redonda, Schele and Peter Mathews, a student at University of Calgary, were the only two conference attendees left at Palenque. Others visited nearby sites that day. Mathews had studied so arduously that he was gaining a visual recognition of important glyphs. When he and Schele walked to the site and stood in front of the monuments that day, it all jived.

"It was like magic," he said.

He saw the signs Eric Thompson, Morley's prize student and later grand master of the Mayanists, had used and applied to the glyphs in the fifties.

On that day with Schele at the pyramids, Mathews' recognition heightened and he became aware of glyphs and signs. He had an epiphany. Rulers' names kept repeating over and over; they kept coming up with Pakal, the greatest lord of Palenque. And they worked out that a Maya sentence began with a date, then a verb, and a person's name. After this realization, they made a series of charts beginning with names and dates. They shared it with the others when they returned that afternoon.

"That was when things began to come together," he said. "It was a turning point."

In *A Forest of Kings*, Freidel states that Proskouria-koff was the lead-in to cracking the code, and that Mayan writing became an abiding part of the American imagination all the way back to Stephens and Catherwood and their Yucatec journey and best selling book.

Which leads us back to breaking the code. Without that, you would not be reading this page, thinking about December 21, 2012, as an end date.

Chapter 3

The Calendars

"The deep time of the Maya calendar is stunning in its scale... It expressed the grandest expressions of time ever put down on stone or paper by human minds ..."
—David Stuart, MacArthur Genius Grant
recipient and archeologist, *The Order of Days: The Maya World and the Truth About It.*

The Maya viewed time in a cyclical rather than a linear manner. Their calendars were not circular in form, but spiral. The present was determined by the past. Everything repeated, everything was a recurring pattern. They only had to view the past to know what would happen in the future. Their intricate system of twenty-eight separate calendars was used for predictions. Most likely they borrowed it from their Mesoamerican neighbors, the Olmec.

Only three calendars were a staple of every day life. This triumvirate includes the *tzolkin*, or sacred round, which lasts 260 days; the *haab,* which is a 360 day "solar" calendar to coordinate with the total number of days it takes the to earth rotate around the sun; and the Long Count Calendar, one of the most important cycles of Maya time, which lasts 5,125 years, and which will end December 21, 2012.

The 260-day *tzolkin* calendar is said to coincide with both the human gestation cycle and the length of time it takes to produce a crop of maize. The count of days, as it is also known, was invented by pairing two smaller cycles—numbers one through thirteen which equals the number of layers in Maya heaven, and the cycle of the twenty "day" names. The *tzolkin* is formed as a circle, not a straight line.

"There is nothing quite like it, anywhere else in the world," says archaeo-astronomer Anthony Aveni, author of **The End of Time: The Maya Mystery of 2012.** "The sacred *tzolkin* is the centerpiece of the Maya calendar system; it is the single most important chunk of time the Maya ever kept, and still keep in remote areas.

"But why 260? Multiply numbers thirteen and twenty? Or two great fertility cycles—those of woman and earth's maize plant? Also the Venus cycle's appearance as morning or evening star is 263 days."

Aveni believes that 260 days came about as some enlightened daykeeper, eons in the past, realized this particular number signified so much.

"It was a focal harmony point. It brought together so many of nature's phenomena: birthing, the moon, Venus, the maize cycle. It may not have come about in a flash," he continues, "but with Maya knowledge that number and nature are joined together perfectly, the discovery of the multiple significance of 260 was bound to be raised to prominence in Maya time consciousness. You even took your name and your fortune from the day name in the 260-day count calendar."

Above all, the *tzolkin* was primarily used for making predictions, for communicating with the gods. The Maya believed a god ruled each day, and depending on that god's traits, it could be good or bad for certain activities. This calendar was used in the way one's horoscope would be viewed today.

The calendar is easy to remember, and that's why it has been passed down and is still in use. It fits into the culture of the people, said Barbara Tedlock, anthropologist and author or *Time and the Highland Maya*.

"It fits into their agriculture, their spinning and weaving. It's something that people use and it doesn't conflict with our calendar. Each day has a characteristic. If today is a 'thought' day, then do something creative; figure out a new design for weaving. People look at the characteristics, the god, of every day. If it's a day that relates to money, then decide to pay bills."

Tedlock should know. She and husband, Dennis Tedlock, widely known for his interpretation of the *Popol Vuh*, the great epic of the Quiché Maya that tells how their forefather gods brought forth the earth from a watery void, were indoctrinated as daykeepers under the formal apprenticeship of a diviner in Momostenango, Guatemala, in the seventies. This is no small undertaking, and daykeepers are recruited in shamanic fashion, with "divine election" through birth, dreams and/or illness.

The Tedlocks had been spending time in various highland Guatemala pueblos, touring churches, asking questions, and a daykeeper divined that they were annoying people at shrines. He told them they had entered the shrines without being ritually clean. A little scared by his remarks, they left the highlands for the city, where Barbara Tedlock became seriously ill. Her illness eventually passed. They returned to Momostenango, renewed contact with the daykeeper, and then were allowed to enter into their apprenticeships. Barbara Tedlock's "divine election" came about through illness.

They settled into village life in Guatemala, became initiated as daykeepers, learned the rituals, and made fewer treks north. As time went on, their contemporaries in the US said they had "gone native."

The *haab* calendar, which works with the *tzolkin,* has eighteen named "months" of twenty calendar days each. The Maya then added five days at the end of this 360-day cycle. It was considered a nineteenth month and these five odd days were considered unlucky but essential to bring a total of 365 days for a full rotation cycle.

These two calendars, like cogs in a wheel, meshed a named day in the *tzolkin* and also had a conjunct day in the *haab.* But this same "double" day could never reproduce again for fifty-two years, roughly the length of a human life. This was called the calendar round, and the only annual time count possessed by the people of Mexico. There were 260 possible different combinations of number and name in this creation.

In this combined calendar round, slippage occurred, because a year is actually 365.24 days, but this didn't bother the Maya. They did not try to play catch up as we do with leap years. They just let time roll along.

"That would mean Christmas could back up to early fall, or the Fourth of July might back up into the cold of winter for us," said Anthony Aveni.

It wasn't of concern to the Maya, Aveni said, because they placed more emphasis on following an unbroken chain of time.

This fifty-two year cycle combination was celebrated throughout Mesoamerica. The Aztecs included it in their new fire ceremony that was timed by sky events. At midnight, when the calendar keepers saw the Pleiades had passed the zenith, they knew the movements of the heavens hadn't stopped and the world wouldn't end and they would have another fifty-two years.

Third in the triumvirate of Maya calendars is the Long Count and although widely used in Mesoamerica, the Maya took it to its highest degree during the classic period. The Long Count consisted of thirteen *baktuns* and lasted 5,125 years. (One *baktun* is 400 years). The starting point of the Long Count calendar, according to early archeologist Eric Thompson, was August 11, 3114 BC. It was known as 4 Ahaw.

This date may have been chosen because it coincided with the completion of a cycle of successful crops, an August summer's day. If you flash forward 5,125 years you come to the cycle's end, and this is where the December 21, 2012 debate comes in. It also ends the thirteenth *baktun* cycle, an auspicious time for the Maya, or 13.0.0.0.0 as carved on Maya stellae.

The Maya, according to Aveni, created the Long Count around 800 BC, "a brilliant invention fashioned out of a huge build-up of base twenty cycles."

Aveni goes on to explain the Maya used this innovation in their calendar so royalty could create a dynastic narrative that covered vast stretches of elapsed time. It extended Maya culture all the way back to the creation of the gods, cementing the reputation of daykeepers and royalty as gods themselves.

The daykeepers act as go-betweens. "They are empowered to make prayers to the gods and ancestors on behalf of the lay people," Barbara Tedlock said.

He or she pays attention to each and every day, making offerings of copal incense and lighting candles. They also do dream interpretations. Through dreams and reading the day's influence, recommendations were then made for the best course of action. Both were used to plot the future.

It's hard for the modern world to fathom why such a complex calendar system existed.

As Michael Coe, archeologist and author of *The Maya, Eighth Edition*, states, "How such a period of time even came into being is an enigma, but the use to which it was put is clear. Every single day had its own omens and associations and the march of the twenty days acted like a fortunetelling machine guiding the destinies of all the Maya and all the peoples of Mexico who used this calendar. It still survives in unchanged form among some indigenous people of southern Mexico and the Maya highlands, under the guard of calendar priests," or daykeepers as Dennis and Barbara Tedlock call them.

With this calendar fashioned as a direct line to the cosmos, royalty and priests were able to govern and control the masses by predicting common events. Most likely with the aid of their calendars and the predictions derived from them, the Maya enjoyed 1500 years of relative stability. It was not until ninth century AD that the Long Count was abandoned and not seen again on Maya stellae.

The Maya Long Count, with 5,125 days, can be compared to the odometer of your car, Aveni says, except instead of tallying miles it clicks off one day at a time in succession. But, when their odometer turns over, the cycle begins anew; your car just goes to the junkyard.

Where did the Maya come up with a beginning date? Researchers think the 'beginning date' of the Long Count was backdated, because the Maya were not keeping time in 3114 BC. They did not surface until around 800 BC.

Though it's agreed that the Long Count is assumed to be Maya, it was shared in all of Mesoamerica and the highest refinement of it came through the classic Maya. The cycles are so long, an event could be fixed so far back in time no one could ever check its authenticity.

When documents were found in the Yucatan in the 1700s, researchers could then coordinate dates in the calendar round with those in the Christian calendar, so Long Count time could then be measured as we measure it. Through these documents it was determined that day zero of the last Maya creation fell on August 11, 3114 BC. Fast forward thirteen *baktuns*, and one arrives at day zero of the next creation, December 21, 2012, the date in question.

Researchers believe these two dates are important because August 11 comes close to the solar zenith passage in southern Maya latitudes, where the Maya calendar was first introduced, and day zero December 21, is winter solstice. On solstice the sun arrives at its maximum southerly position in the sky. It is conceivable that both creation dates are keyed to important positions in the sun cycle.

Maybe the Maya Long Count isn't about ending time, but about the beginning of time and praising the ruler who initiated it, much like our own Gregorian calendar in which case a pope began the great overhaul of how society viewed time. Maybe the Maya weren't that different after all.

~~~~~~

The *tzolkin* is made up of twenty days and the meaning of the Maya days are given below (borrowed from Barbara Tedlock's translation in **Time and the Highland Maya**) from one to twenty in the Yucatec form along with their meaning. Depending on which day you were born, you would receive your name from that named day in the *tzolkin*, and the year from the *haab*. This day-date would not be repeated again for fifty-two years.

Anthropologist Ruth Bunzel said this about the day names, "They are basically twenty sacred word–forces of creation and destruction, good and evil, yielding and immutable, operating in the world, in society and in the heart of man."

1. Imix or water serpent
2. Ik' or wind
3. Ak'bal or night
4. K'an or ripe maize
5. Chikchan or snake
6. Kimi or death
7. Manik or deer
8. Lamat or star
9. Muluk or water jar
10. Ok or dog
11. Chuwen or monkey
12. Eb or tooth
13. Ben or reed
14. Ix or jaguar
15. Men or bird
16. Kib or vulture
17. Kaban or earthquake
18. Etz'nab or knife
19. Kawak or lightning
20. Ahaw or lord

Anthropologist Barbara Tedlock explains, "In the Guatemala highlands, the lower numbers are considered to be gentle or weak, because they are 'newer.'

High numbers, 11, 12 and 13, are violent and middle numbers 7, 8 and 9 are indifferent, neither weak nor violent.

"The latter form the days of measured strength," she states, "which are used for the regularly recurring ceremonies to ensure tranquil life."

The Maya calendars defined who you were, including the depth of your life, possibly the length of your life, the strength of your character, and the state of your future. Simply put, your name day was who you were.

Chapter 4

Gone Viral: Maya Stellae and the 2012 Debate

"Who shall read them?"
—John Lloyd Stephens,
on viewing the Maya stellae
at Copán, Honduras, in 1839.

Stellae: An upright slab placed in the earth, bearing a carved scene or text.

A handful of stellae scattered throughout the Maya world is all that links the final Great Long Count date of the Maya calendar, December 21, 2012, with the doomsday theory proclaiming world's end.

These are Monument 6, Tortuguero, Mexico; Stellae 25, Izapa, Mexico; Stellae 63, Copán, Honduras; Stellae C, Quiriguá, Guatemala; Stellae 1, Cobá, Mexico, and Stellae 5, Cobá, Mexico.

Only Monument 6 refers directly to the end date on which the entire 2012 prophecy hangs. It certainly has the best tale to tell. This monument alone has the end date written in stone—13.0.0.0.0 4 Ahaw, 3 Kankin—which translates to December 21, 2012, the day made popular by the media. According to author David Stuart, *The Order of Days*, this is the only ancient inscription with any clear reference to December 21, 2012, anywhere.

So how did a Maya prophecy come into play? What led scholars, authors and the press to jump on the media bandwagon and make statements that the world was ending in 2012?

Everything rests on Monument 6, which has an unlikely history, one that is barely believable. First of all, it's only a partial monument, really just a broken limestone slab. It was found long after the actual pyramid site had been demolished in Tabasco, Mexico, not far from Palenque.

Decades ago, Tortuguero's temples were wiped out and the stones were removed and used as gravel for construction of a nearby highway. (This may sound odd, but unless you've been to any of the major Mexico pyramid sites, you will never understand the lax manner in which these public treasures are handled). Today a large gravel company occupies the site's original setting. In the sixties a number of issues came to light about this monument.

Monument 6 may have originally resided on an interior temple wall, possibly for the purpose of describing the shrine's ritual significance, according again to Stuart. The actual monument is in at least six fragments. Some pieces were sold off to collectors while others went to a museum in nearby Villahermosa. But photos of each piece exist which allowed archeologists to reconstruct the monument and then come up with a translation.

David Stuart and Stephen Houston were those archeologists. "Only one readable glyph remains and it mentions Maya God Bolon Yokte K'uh, Nine Pole God. He was one of the characters in a group of deities who were 'arranged' on the day of creation, 3114 BC, " said Stuart.

In 1996, Stuart and fellow archeologist Houston published their translation of Monument 6, citing it as the earliest example of Maya predictions for the world's end. According to authors Matthew Restall and Amara Solari in *2012 and the End of the World*, this was because scholars initially speculated the text might be a rare case of Maya prophecy.

A dozen years after Houston and David Stuart speculated that Monument 6 glyphs could be prophetic, Houston issued a rectification and declared it had nothing to do with prophecy; but the dye was cast, and 2012ologists complained that scholars were downplaying Tortuguero's impact because of their fear of 2012 and its allegations.

In 2006, Stuart was asked his opinion of Monument 6, which has the only known reference to 2012.

He offered a quick analysis, he states in his book *The Order of Days*, and posted it to a Mesoamerican studies site, mentioning his take on a glyph next to the name Bolon Yokte K'uh and 'his descent,' as in the descending of a god.

Within weeks, he said, websites around the world reported that his analysis of Monument 6's prophecy was that God Bolon Yokte K'uh will descend. In other words, Stuart's phrase, 'a god was descending,' as good as declared the end times truly were nigh and a savior would return to earth. Many new age writers took this reference and ran with it, creating a new mythology.

After the furor caused by this translation, Stuart then backpedaled and he, too, retracted, stating his descent theory may have been flawed as the glyphs were too broken to read and too difficult for epigraphers to analyze. He is clear, however, that nowhere on the monument does it say that Bolon Yokte K'uh *will* descend at the end of the *baktun* (meaning end date December 21, 2012).

Stuart said Monument 6, in all likelihood, could be passed off as a building dedication, along with Stellae 63, Copán; Stellae 1, Cobá; and Stellae C, Quiriguá: all are building dedications and none prophetic. But John Major Jenkins, front man for the 2012ologists and author of **Maya Cosmogenesis 2012**, maintained if this was a building dedication, then his observations were correct: the Maya viewed house as metaphor for the cosmos.

Stuart retorted that a building was just a building and everything was a huge misunderstanding.

In their book **2012 and the End of the World,** Matthew Restall and Amara Solari state a rough translation of the glyphs might be, "The thirteenth calendrical cycle will end on the date 4 Ahau, the 3rd of Uniiw, when there will occur blackness (or a spectacle) and the god of the nine will come down to the red or be displayed in great investiture." Say what?

Although both Restall and Solari explain this is hardly a clear implication for the end of the world, "With some imagination the text can become an ominous warning, perhaps even apocalyptic.

"It has become one of the sparks, and by some accounts *the* spark, that ignited the firestorm of the 2012 phenomenon."

In **2012 and the End of the World**, it's stated that other ancient sites support the doomsday hypothesis through the alignment of their buildings, as at Izapa, the largest ancient site in Chiapas, Mexico, which was at its heyday from 600 to 100 BC. Though not technically a Maya site, its monuments contain some of the earliest calendrics and illustrations of Maya mythology.

John Major Jenkins claims it is where the Long Count calendar and the 2012 prophecy originated.

Jenkins believes that Stellae 25 encodes a map. He theorizes there is a secret cosmological dimension encoded into Maya mythology. He insists the Maya believed the world would end 2012 AD.

He says the Maya thought a large chapter of human history would be coming to an end, and a new phase of human growth would begin, as in death and rebirth.

He calls it a cyclic renewal of the earth, when a spiritual unfolding of humanity will prevail.

By Jenkins' theory, Stellae 25 at Izapa shows a human supporting a staff with a bird perched on top. At the base lies the head of a caiman bound to a tree, his body extending upward, parallel to the staff. The bird in the tree is supposedly the Big Dipper, or 7 Macaw, and Jenkins says the head of the caiman is the head of the Milky Way or its center. He states the line-up along the local north-south meridian of the great tree that connects bird and beast is mapped out in the night sky as it appeared at midnight, summer solstice, around 300 BC. This was the year Stellae 25 was created. He states this proves the Maya (although Izapa is not a Maya site) were shifting away from a North Polar star-centered region to a southern Milky Way emphasis.

He bases his case on the assumption that Izapa was the place where the galactic solar alignment was first celebrated (his musings) and where he believes the Long Count was formulated. He has created his end of the world doomsday theory on the fact that Izapa monuments fronting the Group F ball court allegedly provide further clues to a 2012 timed creation. He believes in the panorama of the night sky (this theory was originally conceived by Linda Schele in *Maya Cosmos*) a solar deity is canoeing down the Milky Way and a snake-mouthed ball court marker marks the horizon.

Schele, in *Maya Cosmos*, began to consider many scenes from stellae and vases as astronomical interpretations.

"Snakes often represented the ecliptic or the horizon of the solar system along which we perceive the movement of planets and sun," she said in her book.

Jenkins borrows a lot of Schele's imagery from *Maya Cosmos* and makes similar claims. The alignment of the ball court is in line with the horizon and a perfect viewing spot for watching the "canoe" drift through the center of the Milky Way, which is the center of the cosmos. The Milky Way is the mother of creation, says Jenkins; the bulge near the galactic center (constellation of Sagittarius) is the womb or birthplace of the sky. The winter solstice sunrise lines up with the Milky Way and this happens once every 26,000 years, and at Izapa, the Maya told us this eons ago by their positions of some key buildings. Jenkins conveys a lot of imagery, but does it go beyond that?

As Anthony Aveni acknowledges in his book *The End of Time: The Maya Mystery of 2012,* Stellae 25 at Izapa may depict a scene from the *Popol Vuh*, a Maya creation book, in which the hero twins confront the Bird Deity, 7 Macaw (on the stellae) who is the Big Dipper. In her book, *Maya Cosmos*, Schele has a computer generated map of the night sky as it would have appeared in 300 BC, and the Milky Way, which is aligned north and south, appears like the creation scene on Stellae 25, according to Jenkins.

Also, says Jenkins, Group F ball court has a solstice

alignment exact to December's solstice sunset and the June solstice sunrise. On this piece of information he bases most of his theory about the end of the world.

According to archaeo-astronomer Aveni, "It seems a bit risky to pin all of one's conclusions regarding orientation on a single ball court at an early site, and a non-Maya, peripheral one at that."

Next carving in question is Stellae C, Quiriguá, Guatemala, which is linked to the creation of the world through the ruler Cauac Sky. This theory argues in a rather convoluted way, that since it's stated there is a creation, then before creation, there was destruction, or the absence of the world before its creation.

This stellae is one of the few that refers to a creation day, which is 3114 BC in the Maya inscriptions. On that day the first three-stone hearth, the hearth of creation, was lit. Maya narratives speak of planting three stones. Maya hearths were traditionally made up of three stones, and according to Maya scholars Barbara and Dennis Tedlock, the constellation Orion, the hearth, is symbolized by three stones at the bottom of the constellation. Cauac Sky is telling his subjects his kingship is rooted in that moment of creation--all the way back to 3114 BC.

David Stuart is quoted as saying some of the most outrageous calculations into the deep, deep past come from inscriptions on ruins at Quiriguá.

Stellae 63, Copán, Honduras, highlights 9.0.0.0.0 as a calendrical milestone, in year 435 AD, not 2012. One archeologist compares 2012 to our Y2K, with its turn of the millennium importance. He says Stellae 63 at Copán would be like Y1K to the Maya, the shifting at the previous big timeline. The implication is that if 9.0.0.0.0 matters, then 13.0.0.0.0 will matter much more.

Stellae 1 at Cobá contains the oldest date recorded by the Maya. It doesn't limit the year count to five spaces. The scribe continued back twenty-four places to carve a year that consists of twenty thirteen's and four zeros. Stuart asks, in **The Order of Days**, what does it mean?

The same amount of spaces are also used at Stellae 5, Cobá, and he goes on to say these long sequences represent the Long Count calendar at full scale with no shorthand abbreviations. But if one were to take these numbers literally to the endpoint, it would go out some forty-three octillion years by Stuart's math. Using their beginning date of 3114 BC, that would actually lead back twenty-eight octillion years. The Cobá dates show us the full picture of Maya time on a conceptual scale that is nearly incomprehensible.

"So much for saying the calendar ends anytime soon," states Stuart. "It could have been an exercise showing off what could be done with the mathematics of the Long Count. It was recorded on June 28, 672 AD. Both this and Stellae 5 at Cobá mention the base date of the Long Count calendar – 13.0.0.0.0 4 Ahaw 8 Kumku, with twenty four units it reads like this if we were to translate:

13.13.13.13.13.13.13.13.13.13.13.13.13.13.13.13.1 3.13.13.13.0.0.0.0 4 Ahaw 8 Kumku."

In lengthy discourse, archeologist David Stuart argues that this extended repetition means, "The 2012 date of the calendar is not the end of anything, rather it's a mathematically predetermined recurrence of the date of ancient Maya creation. To reiterate, there will be a number of such repetitions in the distant future as well.

"The full Maya calendar encompasses nearly seventy two octillion years from beginning to end. Clearly their conception of time will come to an end eons after our own solar system has burned itself out and the universe is no more.

"No authentic Maya text foretells the end of the world in 2012 or of any destructive event happening in connection with the turn of the thirteenth baktun," finalizes Stuart, in *The Order of Days*.

And lastly where did the idea for 2012 come from? Some say it can be traced to the offhand remark written in 1966 by Michael Coe, professor of anthropology at Yale. Forty years ago he speculated in a book that the upcoming thirteenth *baktun* might have been thought of as an "Armageddon" that would see the destruction of the world.

In making this claim, he was drawing upon mythic history used elsewhere in Mesoamerica, most notably from the Aztecs' cycles of world destruction and creation. And Coe admits then as now, no Maya source makes any such claim to 2012, he was simply speculating about the ways in which the ancient Maya conceived of that important date in their calendar.

Even though it's only been possible to read Maya hieroglyphs for the past two decades, the impact of those readings has been enormous. Slowly the image of the ancient Maya has come to life, now by their own words. Let's just hope we mere mortals can manage to translate them accurately.

Chapter 5

2012ologists: Who, What, Why?

"2012 is a new chance to recreate our world."
—Website Chichen2012.org.

It wasn't until the late nineties that I started to hear about the last day scenario of the Maya calendar. That phenomenon gained steam with John Major Jenkins' 1998 book, *Maya Cosmogenesis 2012.* Jenkins was one of the frontrunners promoting the Maya calendar end date, after being influenced by Jose Argüelles, author of *The Mayan Factor: Path Beyond Technology* and Linda Schele, iconographer, and author of *Maya Cosmos.*

Argüelles, now deceased, was also at the head of the class of New Age thinkers who trumpeted 2012's prophecy. Argüelles was influenced by Frank Waters, author of *Mexico Mystique, the Coming Sixth World of Consciousness*, which laid groundwork for the current thread linking 2012 with the end of time.

A blending of Jenkins, Argüelles and Waters has given us 2012ology, as it's been coined. To date, a huge compilation of books, blogs and documentaries has been churned out with 2012 in mind.

John Major Jenkins has been the front man for the 2012 movement ever since his book came out. Along with Schele's influence, a trip to Tikal, Guatemala, in 1986 also played an important role in Jenkin's 2012 coming of age.

After years of research, he formulated a theory about the Maya calendar's Long Count, which operates separately from the *tzolkin*, their sacred calendar. The Long Count lasts a cycle of 5,125 years composed of 13 *baktuns*. (Each *baktun* lasts about 400 years).

In the Long Count the Maya calculated that from its beginning (which was backdated to 3114 BC) the end date would be winter solstice 2012, December 21. Jenkins looked at astrology charts for those dates to see the configurations of planets, but decided this didn't pack enough punch to constitute what might occur at the end of the Long Count calendar. In essence, astrology was weak tea in comparison to the kind of association Jenkins was trying to correlate with an important end-times date.

What actually happens on December 21, 2012? A rare astronomical event will occur: the sun conjuncts the intersection of the Milky Way and the plane of the ecliptic. The Milky Way extends north and south in the night sky. The ecliptic is the path the sun, moon, planets and stars appear to travel in the sky from east to west. This intersection of the sun and the Milky Way is at a sixty-degree angle near the constellation Sagittarius. This cosmic cross is called the sacred tree to the Maya.

This occurrence, known as the precession of the equinoxes, happens once every 25,800 years. It occurs due to the wobble in the earth's axis that was caused by an astral object, maybe a meteor, hitting our planet sometime in the long distant past. Because of the wobble, the winter solstice sunrise has been slowly moving toward this galactic center.

To paraphrase Jenkins, he felt the Mayans noticed the slippage of the positions of stars in the night sky over long periods of observation, and their calendar foretold of the coming attraction. By using the Long Count the Mayans did the math and anchored the date December 21, 2012, as the end of their Great Long Count cycle.

For this once-in-a-26,000-year event to be noted by the Maya, they would have had to be aware of the precession. Archeologist David Stuart, in **The Order of Days**, says that's impossible, that the precession has only been detected recently.

But there is data that Hipparchus, a Greek astronomer, made the first discovery of precession in 128 BC. So if the Greeks were aware of precession, it's entirely possible that the Maya knew of it, too.

Due to the earth's wobble, precession gives the impression that the sun rises against the background of different constellations as the centuries elapse. The result is that the equinox sun will soon be rising in the constellation of Aquarius rather than Pisces. Jenkins says we are moving out of the Age of Pisces into the Age of Aquarius. But since these ages can lap two hundred plus years (the actual Age of Aquarius will not happen until 2300), he felt the Maya Long Count calendar was onto something bigger than even that.

In another book that helped shape 2012ology, **Hamlet's Mill,** by Giorgio de Santillana and Hertha von Dechen, there's reference to "the celestial frame of time wherein precession has a primary influence on the changing destinies of humankind."

The authors wrote that 6400 years ago (4400 BC) the autumn equinox sun coincided with the Milky Way and this led to a fabled Golden Age, as acknowledged in many myths.

"This was a time when the sun, in conjunction with

the Milky Way during the fall equinox, caused a harmonious alignment to exist in the sky, and be showered on the planets and sun below."

But then as precession happened due to the wobble, this favorable alignment became inconjunct, and change occurred. After a few millennia of a mother worship culture by our stone-age ancestors, when peaceful co-existence was the norm, around 4400 BC a patriarchal system took front and center position, which was the forerunner to our western tradition of dominance today.

In **Hamlet's Mill**, authors de Santillana and von Dechen discuss how ancient myths proclaim a future time when cosmic harmony will return to the earth. And the Maya keyed into this.

So fast-forward to December 2012. The world has gone through four millennia of strife, but as winter solstice 2012 nears, this very rare alignment will occur. December solstice is the traditional beginning of earth's yearly cycle. Many 2012ologists believe the Maya timed their Long Count to coincide with an event being recognized as a rare world age shift and this area of the sky where all these symbols and celestial objects converge is the center of our own Milky Way galaxy.

The Maya believed the world would be reborn. The **Popol Vuh**, a Maya book of mythology that can be compared to our Bible, told tales of the earth being destroyed several times before its present incarnation. They were no strangers to the theory that worlds ended when cycles were complete so that humanity could remake itself and continue on.

Jenkins believes the Maya left a code behind, and he is determined to locate that code. He toured Mexico's ancient ruins and locked in on the west coast site of Izapa. Much of his 2012olgy debate is based on Stellae

25 that pictures a human figure supporting a staff with a bird on top (see Chapter 4). At the base of the staff lies an alligator bound to a tree. His body extends upward parallel to the staff. The bird in the tree is supposedly the Big Dipper or Seven Macaw to the Maya. The head of the alligator is the Milky Way, or its center in our constellation Sagittarius, where the bulge of the Milky Way is located.

The lineup along the meridian of the great cosmic tree that connects bird and beast is allegedly mapped out on the sky as it appeared at midnight when the stellae was erected in 300 BC. Much of this theory has been borrowed from Linda Schele's *Maya Cosmos*.

Jenkins believes the scene represents a Maya cosmic clue left to the world, a mystery to be unraveled. Even though Izapa was not a Maya site, Jenkins still uses this as his basis.

He theorizes that the affect at the moment of alignment will mark an entry into a new world age that could transform our consciousness "into a collective earth spirit...if we are ready for it."

Jenkins believes we can come through the end date renewed and realigned, bringing galactic wisdom with us along the way.

~~~~~

An even more profound influence on the Maya 2012 debate was Jose Argüelles. The author, who died in March 2011, was best known for *The Mayan Factor, Path Beyond Technology*, published in 1987.

Argüelles founded the harmonic convergence movement in August 1987, based in part on his rendering of the Maya calendar.

His take on the Maya reads like an exciting science fiction thriller, with the abandonment of sites at the height of their classic age relating to that of the Hopi myth, regarding the mysterious red city of the south. In this story concerning Hopi migrations, a city is built and on completion, the Hopi are instructed to abandon it, leaving it as a memorial to knowledge.

Argüelles believed that myth quantified the Maya. Their purpose, he said, was to codify and establish a system of knowledge, and after putting it down in stone and text, move along.

As Argüelles painted, wrote and meditated, he began to look at the Maya culture in a new light. He began to formulate a theory after discovering Ben Franklin's Magic Square of Eight, which yields the sum of 260, the exact number of days in the Maya *tzolkin* calendar. This, along with his studies of the I-Ching, led him to publish **Earth Ascending,** and right after that he began to consider the nature of UFOs and extra-terrestrial intelligence. He believed information could be transmitted through light or radiant energy.

Argüelles happened upon Maya daykeeper Hunbatz Man. I also had the opportunity to meet Hunbatz when he came to Puerto Morelos in 1999 where he lectured on the end date of the Maya calendar. Hunbatz now heads a huge 2012 cult that leads followers from city to city throughout the US to chant and meditate. When I sat in on his lecture in Puerto Morelos, he declared the end date would result in a "shifting of the poles north and south, and vast destruction."

In **The Maya Factor**, Argüelles explains how three archeologists--Goodman, Martinez-Hernandez and Thompson--who worked out that the Long Count cycle began August 11, 3114 BC and the same date would again occur December 21, 2012, had correlated the beginning of the Great Cycle. This would tally thirteen *baktuns* of roughly 400 years each.

He theorized the Maya appeared 300 AD at Uaxactun, spreading to classic sites Tikal, Palenque, Copán and Quiriguá by 500 AD. For the next 300 years, and the duration of *baktun* 9, they built stepped pyramids and left behind stellae with recorded dates every five, ten, twenty years. Then in 830 AD came their decline and by the end of the tenth century, they mingled with the Toltecs, took on the concept of Quetzalcoatl/Kukulkan, and built up Uxmal and Chichen Itza.

No more stone recordings occurred, or astronomical data. Warfare was on the rise as was human sacrifice and they developed the League of Mayapan, very unlike what they did before when things were apolitical for the classic Maya. Mayapan fell in 1441, and by the time the Spaniards arrived in the Yucatan in 1527, there was total disunity. The existing texts that survived, **Chilam Balam** and **Popol Vuh**, were written after the conquest and give no information about their classic Maya predecessors.

Here's where it gets interesting. Argüelles believed these classic Maya centers were cosmic calling cards from elsewhere in the cosmos. Their planetary cycles were correlated as a matrix that encompassed thirteen numbers and twenty symbols, the Maya *tzolkin* calendar dynamics.

Argüelles believed the Maya were a people founded on the principle of harmonic resonance, possibly harking back to his own harmonic convergence theory. They placed the earth in resonance with the sun, as an evolving member of a larger galactic family. The Maya, he said, were the link with the galactic universe, and through the pyramids built in 9 *baktun,* they gave the earth a plan for the galaxy to align itself.

The *tzolkin* is the cosmic code, the simplest possible mathematical matrix to accommodate the largest possible number of harmonic transformations and transmissions—it's a "table" of galactic frequencies.

Argüelles' engaging concept was that the Maya are galactic space travelers, scouting out star systems looking for potential alignment with the cosmic whole. The Maya, diviners of harmony, are on the roam. Backed on what premise? Well, that's the question.

Once a system is surveyed and monitored, if it has evolutionary potential for harmonic attainment (but by whom?) the Maya make it ready for the final adjustments.

The Maya transmit themselves, somehow, through the DNA code, like maximum velocity Star Trekkers beaming through the galactic ether, "from one star system to another."

According to Argüelles's book, **The Mayan Factor**, "with a science based on the principle of resonant harmonics, they could translate whole number mathematics into wave structures of different frequencies and transmit the information."

Argüelles was exquisitely far out. He was the antithesis of modern archeologists like Coe or Stuart. He saw the Maya as cosmic space travelers who left us a road map to galactic alignment that will only be possible at sunrise on December 21, 2012.

Like a science fiction thriller, they had one *baktun* (400 years) and one *baktun* only to establish and build the elaborate stepped pyramids that were road maps to divinity, or as Argüelles called it, harmonic resonance.

Through art studies including collage and sumi ink painting, and esoteric studies which included I Ching, Chinese Taoism, Tibet Buddhism and meditation through master Chogyam Trungpa Rinpoche, Arguelles developed his theory. He was partial to information he gleaned from Frank Waters' *Mexico Mystique,* and Laurette Sejourne's book *Burning Water: Thought and Religion in Ancient Mexico.*

He relied mostly, however, on the Hopi myth of the mysterious red city of the south, built solely for gaining knowledge before it was abandoned. Argüelles compared Maya pyramids and their abandonment at the height in the ninth century to the Hopi myth.

That myth was to codify and establish a system of knowledge and then move along. He said since they were so concerned with "cycles of time, understanding time as a qualitative bearer of the conditions of cosmic or galactic seasons, they saw a period of gathering darkness on the horizon and for that reason knew it was time to call it quits and check out."

Given the condition of the world today, who is to say that they weren't correct? Argüelles argued.

The premises of these 2012ologists, Argüelles and Jenkins, are the foundation on which the entire end-times debate rests. Worthy theories? You be the judge.

Chapter 6

The Milky Way and the Precession of the Equinoxes

Night sky Milky Way
Naked eye astronomy
Maya stellar sight.
—Maya haiku

We all know what the Milky Way is, but what is the precession of the equinoxes?

Precession takes place when the winter solstice sun rises in conjunction with the center of the galaxy. It's the slow move along the ecliptic of the vernal equinox.

What is the ecliptic? The ecliptic is the line of constellations in which the sun rises and sets throughout the year. We divide it into twelve zodiacal signs. (The Maya divided it into thirteen). At night these ecliptic constellations create a path across the sky that marks the track of the sun in its daily and yearly movement. From month to month different constellations dominate the night sky due to precession. The moon and planets also follow this path that snakes back and forth again as the year proceeds.

What causes precession? The sun and moon want the equator to line up with the ecliptic plane. The earth resists these forces by gyrating or wobbling like a top. One cycle of gyration takes approximately 26,000 years.

"Because the axis of the earth wobbles a bit," said Linda Schele in **Maya Cosmos**, "the sun migrates through one constellation on the ecliptic every two thousand years or so. This shift changes the times a particular constellation would pass the zenith on a particular night or which form of the Milky Way would be visible at a chosen hour."

In other words, hour-by-hour, the night sky we see now is different than the sky viewed by the ancient Maya a millennia or more ago. Constellations shift over time.

Due to the wobble, precession shows up in the drift of stars where the celestial pole is situated, also. As centuries glide by, we get a different North Pole star. Today it is Polaris, five thousand years ago it was Thurban, and in the future, it will change to Vega.

So what do the Milky Way and the precession of the equinoxes have to do with the Maya?

New Age thinkers believe the winter solstice of 2012 represents a rare alignment in precession with the solstice and the galaxy and that is why the Maya chose this end date.

One 2012ologist in particular, John Major Jenkins, feels ancient cultures believed in the idea of periodic shifting world ages. The ancients followed the night sky and thought it was linked to the changing structures in humanity.

He feels that the mystery of the ages is solved in the astronomical fact of the precession of the equinoxes, and ancient sky watchers, like the Maya, observed the solstice sun and the Milky Way coming closer together. They would have viewed this as a synchronization that would happen in a future epoch.

That epoch is literally happening on December 21,

2012, after a cycle of nearly 26,000 years. Jenkins and others believe the Maya calculated when this would occur and encoded it into their Long Count calendar. Our sun, or star, will be perfectly aligned with the center of the Milky Way.

Many believe the Maya were aware of the world ages that authors de Santillana and von Dechen write about in **Hamlet's Mill**. They faithfully recorded the activities of the night skies to put meaning to their existence. They believed in predictions, and in cycles of time, and that the past always returned at some time in the future. By recording the sky's activities, they would know when to expect the 'expected.' This means they would have known that the plane of the ecliptic and the Milky Way would intersect on a date in the far future, thus ushering in either mayhem or change for the better.

But did the Maya observe the precession of the equinoxes? In putting this claim to others who've studied the Maya 2012 phenomenon, many question whether or not the Maya were aware of it.

According to Anthony Aveni, author of **The End of Time: The Maya Mystery of 2012**, "Precession is one of the longest astronomical cycles and the fountainhead of many theories based on cosmic determinism, or ideas to link human destiny with the cosmos. That this 26,000 year cycle just happens to add up to five of their Long Count cycles has added fuel to the fire that in their quest for cosmic harmony, the Maya may have stumbled upon one of the grandest of all celestial cycles."

But this does not prove the Maya were aware of it. Aveni says there's no evidence to suggest they developed coordinate systems based on the ecliptic or the equator, nor did they use geometry. But he believes one area where it could prove they utilized it was in the astronomical alignments of Maya architecture. They aligned certain special buildings to horizontal positions of both the sun and Venus, as at Izapa.

Did other world cultures know about precession? It was originally 'discovered' by the Greek Hipparchus in 128 BC after he spent years tabulating the position of 850 stars in celestial longitude and latitude based on data recorded by his predecessors of the previous two centuries.

The Chinese knew about precession according to written records from 330 AD. It's thought that the Egyptians and the Babylonians were aware of it, also. So why not the Maya? We know they devised a zodiac (theirs had thirteen signs rather than twelve) so they were concerned with the movement of the sun and planets along the ecliptic. Although they left no records of coordinates based on the ecliptic or the equator, some 2012ologists believe, as does Aveni, they left evidence of their awareness of precession by the alignment of architecture at certain sites.

On to the Milky Way and how the Maya viewed it. The Milky Way in its north-south position becomes the World Tree to the Maya. It is also the road, or *Sac-Be*, to the underworld for dead souls as well as the path for those souls to the sky. On the sarcophagus lid of Pakal, Palenque's greatest ruler, there is a representation of the king descending down the World Tree into the jaws of *Xibalba*, the underworld, to his death.

"The greatest of the Classic Maya portals to the Otherworld is also found in the night sky," said Schele.

Schele and Freidel's hypothesis in **Maya Cosmos**, is that the Milky Way--portrayed as a tree--stood in the middle of the cosmos in perfect north–south alignment on the last day of the previous creation, as shown in the figure of the sky map.

On Creation Day, August 11, 3014 BC, sunset started with the Milky Way taking the position of the World Tree, but turning into the angled position of the Crocodile Tree, a very ancient image for the Maya, in the two hours after dusk when the sky became dark. This reverts back to the Maya creation myth from the ancient text, the **Popol Vuh**, where the hero twins confront cosmic bird, 7 Macaw (the Big Dipper), which is carved on Stellae 25 at Izapa.

"This was one of the final actions that prepared the old universe for the creation of the new," said Schele

So the World Tree becomes the road to the underworld, or the *Sac-Be*, and on December 21, 2012, our sun will be positioned to dive right into its very center.

Chapter 7

Collapse of the Maya

"Too many farmers grew too many crops
on too much of the landscape."
—David Webster, *The Fall of the Ancient Maya:
Solving the Mystery of the Maya Collapse.*

Why did the Maya abandon their pyramids and ceremonial centers in the ninth century AD? What caused the collapse of the Maya civilization?

Although the fall of the Maya isn't directly related to the 2012 end date, it's a controversial subject that lends itself to debate. The romantic notion of a mystical civilization that disappeared into the jungle after erecting grand pyramids may in part be responsible for the high level of interest in the Maya prophecy. Why? Maybe we want to believe this mysterious lost culture had more of a take on our position in the universe than we do. Maybe we think they left us secret codes carved on ancient stone tablets. Maybe because they were an indigenous, otherworldly people, we believe they could perceive cosmic truths that we cannot.

Many reasons have been thrown around to explain the collapse of the Classic Maya including wars, disease, overpopulation, and finally, drought. Most scholars believe a combination of these led to their fall, but one notable scholar believes drought, and drought alone, caused their downfall.

According to Michael Coe in **The Maya, Eighth Edition**, researchers discovered a major drought that corresponded to the lapse between the early and late classic periods--a time when no new stellae were erected and in which earlier stellae were defaced. Defacing stellae can be compared to graffiti writing on buildings today. It shows lack of respect for those in authority. The Maya civilization was on the wane and it would be a slow demise for another five hundred years.

Recent testing of skeletal remains at various Maya sites shows evidence of disease and malnutrition right across the board—in both nobles and peasants. Use of slash and burn agriculture caused land exhaustion and deprived the ground of nutrients. As a response to overpopulation the peasants increased intensive farming techniques in an attempt to literally feed the masses. Their production system may have just become overburdened, said Coe. There wasn't enough food to go around. The Maya apocalypse had ecological roots; they exploited the land on which they lived.

Although peasant-farmers made up eighty percent of Maya society they were unable to support a growing mass of non-farmers because of agricultural limitations. Due to lack of flat, farmable land, they couldn't grow wheat and instead grew corn. Corn, their main staple, has a much lower protein content than wheat. It was impossible to store corn for longer than a year due to the humid conditions on both the Yucatan Peninsula and in the lowlands, so they couldn't make it through a drought that lasted longer than a year. And finally, they had few edible domestic animals—only turkeys and ducks—no cows or sheep. The Maya grew to the point that the agrarian society couldn't support the urban residents in their city-states. As it was, the Maya cities were "already economically fragile," according to author Richardson Gill, in *The Great Maya Droughts: Water, Life and Death.* As the population grew, even a month's drought could be devastating.

In *The Maya, Eighth Edition*, Coe categorizes the research of three University of Florida scientists who took samples of sediment from Lake Punta Laguna near Cobá. Their study details climate patterns for the Maya lowlands for 3500 years. The most dramatic finding showed evidence of an unusually severe drought from 850 AD to 1050 AD, peaking at 862 AD. This was one of the driest periods to be recorded in over three millennia. Coe concludes that conditions of an extreme two hundred year drought and year after year of lower crop production lead pipe cinched the Maya collapse.

One by one the lights of the Classic Maya civilization went out, and the very last known inscription date carved on their stellae was 910 AD in the Peten. In prosperous times stellae recorded major events detailing triumphs of kings and defeats of enemies. From roughly 900 AD there was either nothing to report or no backing for it, meaning there was a chink in the Maya armor. The kings could not maintain prosperity and when rains didn't come and crop harvests were not large enough to feed the population, disillusionment set in.

Peace was dependent on a Maya ruler who could preside over the temples and could also function as a high priest. It was his responsibility to pray to the gods, perform astronomical and calendar rituals and ensure timely arrival of rains on which their agriculture depended. Their ruler claimed he had the power to deliver the goods and asserted he was as supernatural as the gods. Of course, if he failed to meet his end of the agreement, his subjects could revolt. The sacking and destruction of stellae at various sites shows that the Maya masses may have learned their emperor was not wearing any clothes.

According to Jared Diamond, author of **Guns, Germs, and Steel: The Fates of Human Societies**, it's amazing how many cultures do collapse and one of history's disturbing facts is that collapse is caused by the destruction of the natural resources on which these cultures depend. The Anasazi, Easter Islanders, the kingdom of Angkor Wat in Cambodia... and the Maya. These civilizations and many others succumbed to various combinations of environmental degradation and climate change, aggressive enemies taking advantage of their resulting weakness, and declining trade with neighbors who faced their own environmental problems. Because peak population, wealth and resource consumption are accompanied by peak environmental impact, approaching the limit at which impact outstrips resources, we can now understand why declines of societies tend to swiftly follow their peaks, Diamond reported.

Oddly enough, Maya agrarian success may have set the stage for its eventual collapse. Timing being everything, the Maya rise was facilitated by a rainy period that began 250 BC and lasted until 125 AD; this was the early beginning of their rise to power. Temporary droughts over the next few centuries were weathered; one was associated with a pre-Classic collapse at some sites. Another collapse came at Tikal, Guatemala, around 600 AD when there was a drought. But in 750 AD the worst drought in thousands of years began. This has been deemed the true cause of the collapse.

This monstrous drought most affected the southern highlands as it had the densest population and the least amount of water available because of a high water table.

The southern highlands lost more than ninety nine percent of its population during the Classic collapse. When Cortes marched through in 1524, an area that had previously been inhabited by millions of Maya, he nearly starved because so few villagers were around to supply him corn.

Once the drought came, insult was added to injury, as increased fighting became the norm with more people scrapping over fewer resources. It's known that Maya warfare peaked just before the collapse. More than five million people –mostly farmers-- were crammed into an area the size of the state of Colorado. And although the Maya were no strangers to drought, this one was the most severe. With previous droughts they could just move to another area, but by the time of the Classic collapse, there was no useful unoccupied land to which they could move.

Because the Maya population had expanded so greatly, it was necessary for them to utilize all their major resources to survive. Archeologists took measurements of the size of trees before the Classic era, and discovered they were much longer, wider, and higher quality woods than in the post Classic era. Old growth forests had been leveled as the Maya culture expanded and their cities grew.

But destruction of forests tends to create decreased or lowered rainfall. Deforestation can cause manmade drought. To try and bolster up crops for a burgeoning population's needs, the Maya mismanaged their environment by overplanting, using slash and burn agriculture, and by cutting their forests for housing and fuel. Then when no rains came, the peasants lost faith in their warrior priests and abandoned the cities; their farming techniques could no longer support the growing population. But, according to Gill in **The Great Maya Droughts**, no tears were shed.

Although much of their civilization was probably lost, the ecological refugees, he said, disillusioned by their high priests and kings, left the cities and departed for the north, taking with them the best of the urban culture—art, medicine and rituals—that had developed over 1500 years.

Wars, revolutions and disease do not make a powerful nation fall, but lack of water—in the form of a two hundred year drought-- will do it every time.

Chapter 8

Prophecy

"Time is adjusting itself. We've completed many cycles.
We cannot call it an end of time, year zero.
Time continues on; it is infinite."
—Maria Faviana Chochoy Alva, Maya elder,
in the documentary, *2012: The True Mayan Prophecy*.

And so we come to the prophecy. Is December 21, 2012 the end of the world? Did the Maya know the world had a limited shelf life and are we ignoring it? Or is winter solstice 2012 just another day? Here's another question. How did the idea of an end date fast track its way into the media? Why the ruckus?

We know the Maya calendar's Great Long Count will be complete on December 21, 2012. It's the end of a 5,125 year cycle, also known as the thirteen *baktuns*, a very important time for the Maya. But why is this meaningful to us? If the Maya code had not been broken a couple decades ago, we wouldn't even know that an end date to the Long Count calendar existed.

Because the code was indecipherable for more than a century and the Maya conveyed such mystery for so long, has too much importance been placed on every little thing Maya?

It looks like we have author and archeologist Michael Coe to blame in part for the great December 21, 2012 debate. In **The Maya** (1966) he wrote, "When the great cycle of the Long Count reaches completion on the final day of the thirteenth cycle, our present universe will be annihilated."

This was the first mention of an apocalypse. What a choice of words, and words that were pounced on by the New Age media. Although Coe has since retracted his statement, along with his prognostication, others have chimed in.

The original idea of a Maya prophecy, however, may have begun with author Frank Waters, known as the grandfather of Southwestern literature. He wrote **The Book of the Hopi,** and followed it in 1971 with **Mexico Mystique: The Coming Sixth World of Consciousness,** from which many of the current threads of 2012 thinking can be traced. He suggested ancient Mesoamerican deities reflected "a universal meaning that is as pertinent now as it was two thousand years ago."

He incorrectly fused together both Aztec and Maya belief systems, incorporating the Maya creation date of 3014 BC with what is known to the Aztecs as the fifth sun. And he can be thanked for stating the close of the "Great Cycle" thirteenth *baktun* in 2012 would mean the world's end, destruction by earthquakes, which he based on the Aztec sun legend.

The main problem with Waters' premise is that he created a potpourri of cultures--Hopi, Maya and Aztec—his own amalgamation tossed into one. A major bone of contention with the 2012ologists' theories is that they've picked and chosen from many plates.

According to David Stuart in **The Order of Days,** "It was Water's collapsing of two or more different mythical narratives that helped light the spark of the 2012 movement."

Waters directly influenced author Jose Argüelles, *The Mayan Factor.* Argüelles claimed to be the Messenger of the Command of Pacal Votan, stating the Maya were galactic agents who'd come to earth in order to "place earth and its solar system in synchronization with the larger galactic community. The 2012 date bodes nothing less than a major evolutionary upgrading of the light-life-radiogenetic-process which our planet represents."

Argüelles, who died in March 2011, was best known for the Harmonic Convergence event that was to occur in 1987. This was based on his understanding of the Maya calendar that he assumed "would usher in a new era energized by world peace and harmony and a rejection of war and strife."

Yes, we would all like to see these things come about. We may have missed it in 1987, but 2012ologists believe we are still on track to catch that brass ring. Daniel Pinchbeck wrote *2012: the Return of Quetzalcoatl*, and threw in the Maya along with Quetzalcoatl, more a central Mexican deity than singularly Maya.

Quetzalcoatl is a savior figure who returns to bring salvation to the world, thereby extending the descending god theory of Monument 6 at Tortuguero. Pinchbeck came to his conclusions through hallucinogenic visions he had with Amazon tribes while in South America.

The premise would hold more water if a tribesman or shaman from, say, a Central American country, theorized his findings while on a spiritual quest rather than a first world author who'd flown into the rainforest to partake of the local hallucinogens. I believe there is such a thing as collective unconscious, but why are people other than the Maya touting most if not all 2012 calendar predictions?

The most prominent voice of the New Age 2012 debate is John Major Jenkins. He says the Maya predicted a change from "one extreme form of social organization to another" with the turn of the *baktun* period offering an opening of consciousness and "a creative participation with the earth process that gives birth to our higher selves."

He focuses on astronomical symbols and carvings and architectural layouts at the ruins of Izapa. He claims the monuments at the site are the foundation of the 2012 prophecies and spiritual teachings "that apply to end cycle endings."

To him, the Maya date is "a true and accurate artifact of the Mayan philosophy of time."

Jenkin's specific claim is that on December 21, the sun will rise in direct alignment with the center of the Milky Way galaxy and that the Maya were aware of this future occurrence. He maintains the 2012 date is the end point of a complete precession cycle of 26,000 years.

This is a sticking point that archeologists and scholars have with the predictions of the 2012ologists. New Agers rely on the Maya being aware of two key points: our sun's placement in the center of the galaxy on December 21 and the precession of the equinoxes. David Stuart flatly refuses to believe the Maya knew about precession, contradicting John Major Jenkins' belief that "the sun will rise in direct alignment with the center of the Milky Way galaxy and the Maya were aware of this."

Jenkins emphasizes that 2012 is the end point of a complete precession cycle of which the Maya had some knowledge and were able to predict.

Stuart says Jenkins is dead wrong in *The Order of*

Days. "Not the least of which is that the Maya could have had any idea of a galactic center in the first place. The center of the Milky Way was recognized by modern science only a few decades ago through the methods developed in radio astronomy."

Scholars in general say the Maya are not focused on the apocalyptic. "Conspicuous in its absence in any of the written records at Palenque or elsewhere is any mention of what comes next at the opposite of creation; at the end of everything. Given all the current interest in how the ancient Maya are said to have predicted an end of the world, or how they knew their calendar would end in 2012, this might come as something of a surprise."

But spiritualists and New Age devotees have latched onto the Maya as a people aware of an ancient form of wisdom that can predict the future. Many scholars believe New Age writers are to blame for the hype.

David Friedel, co-author of *A Forest of Kings,* firmly believes the Maya did not consider this to be the end of creation. He notes that Pakal, Palenque's greatest ruler, predicted in his inscriptions that the 80th calendar round anniversary of his accession would be celebrated eight days after the first eight thousand year cycle when the Maya calendar ends October 15, 4772.

And the Maya scribe who carved Stellae C at Quirguá, says Stuart, would see the end of a cycle as simultaneously the start of a new one if he were recording dates today.

"Many people today see the ancient Long Count calendar as having a profound relevance on our own modern world, as a mechanism that predicted an upcoming end of times or a transformation of consciousness...The truth of the matter is that the Maya calendar was inseparable from the ancient world that created it: a lost worldview of kings, gods and ancestors. By wrenching this special vision of time and cosmology away from that particular cultural and historical milieu, we do nothing more than manipulate the past for our own purposes and messages."

~~~~~~~

What do the modern Maya have to say about December 21, 2012? Is it a paradigm shift or resetting the clock? Cataclysm or rebirth? Some present day Maya endorse the concept that the 2012 end date has critical importance while others are not even aware of it, and some think it has no significance at all. Some Maya believe we are in a period of transition; others say it is just another cycle.

Rigoberta Menchú Tum, Nobel Prize laureate and author of *I, Rigoberta Menchú*, a Quiché Maya from the Guatemala highlands who was forced to leave her country during the heinous years of the Guatemala government's disappearing thousands of indigenous Maya, said, "There are a lot of people speaking for the Maya with little respect for the sacred Mayan calendar or the culture.

"For us, the Maya, during this phase, time does not exist. Time is completely dispersed. It is 'disordered time,' when the greatest breakdown of humanity will occur, plagued by loneliness, stress and fear.

"For humanity, it is the hardest and darkest of times...Humanity is being called to a great responsibility, affected by our actions. We call them natural disasters but they are not natural. Much pain is already occurring.

"The Maya elders say if we do not take right actions, today, one-quarter of the people of the earth could perish."

For the documentary film **2012: The True Mayan Prophecy**, Dawn Engle and Ivan Suvanjieff, founders of the non-profit organization PeaceJam, interviewed modern Maya in various walks of life, including Maya elders. Needless to say, the responses received were a mixed bag, not unlike the inconsistencies found between archeologists and 2012ologists regarding the 2012 end date.

Menchú Tum, who is interviewed in the film, said we're living in a moment of chaos and though there is global disorder right now, 2012 will usher in a more balanced period, if only we allow it.

"A new time is drawing near, so it is important to maintain the light shining in these days, our personal light and our collective light. And we need to reflect on what can be done and try to visualize what we are actually doing, because without meaning to, sometimes we contribute to negative aspects of life.

"We are passing through an era of disordered time which began in 1992 and will last forty years. There are things that happen that are not merely caused by people," she said. "It is the age, the energy, the cosmos."

In the film, Menchú Tum introduces her spiritual advisors, Maria Faviana Chochoy Alva and Pedro Celestino Yac Noy. They say that apocalyptic predictions misrepresent the meaning of the end of the Maya Long Count cycle (known as the thirteenth *baktun*). Their position is that this will be a time of great transition.

The years leading up to the end of the thirteenth *baktun* and the start of the new cycle have been years of struggle as people are more detached from each other and from nature.

Chochov Alva says we must remember, "We are born into our mother's womb plus the womb of Mother Earth, and we are all brothers and sisters. We are each one more child of Mother Earth."

Menchú Tum also emphasizes that we must understand we are connected, and that we have broken from Mother Nature and we've also been cut off from Mother Nature, and that is making us sick, both mentally and physically. We need to be reconnected; the energies of nature are healing and curing. The source of life is infinite and continual, and abundance is already ours.

What actions can we take to survive this transition? Menchú Tum and her advisors suggest a five-fold plan: resist the vortex of fear, anger, hate and negativity; guard your health—both physically and mentally; reconnect with your spiritual roots and try to fill the void within; find your mission, play your role, and be a shining light to others; and most important of all, they stress, help heal our Mother Earth.

This is the real meaning, the true Maya prophecy, of December 21, 2012.

In the documentary, Menchú Tum says, "An era of 5,125 years is coming to a close. It will launch a brand new era. In this era, for the very first time, male and female energies will be united.

"My greatest hope is life itself. I believe that life endures even through the different ages of humanity. I believe life will carry on."

Bienvenidos à December 21, 2012.

Bibliography

The following books and articles were helpful as resource material:

Argüelles, José. *The Mayan Factor, Path Beyond Technology, Revised Edition*. Santa Fe: Bear & Company, 1996.

Aveni, Anthony. *The End of Time, The Maya Mystery of 2012*. Boulder: University Press of Colorado, 2009.

Coe, Michael D. *Breaking the Maya Code*. New York: Thames and Hudson, 1993.

Coe, Michael D. *The Maya*. New York: Thames and Hudson, 1966.

Coe, Michael D. *The Maya, Eighth Edition, Ancient People and Places*. New York: Thames and Hudson, 1966.

De Santillana, Giorgio and Hertha von Dechen. *Hamlet's Mill: An Essay Investigating Human Knowledge and Its Origin Through Myth*. Jaffrey, New Hampshire: David R. Godine, 1992.

Demarest, Arthur. *Ancient Maya: The Rise and Fall of a Rainforest Civilization*. Cambridge: Cambridge University Press, 2004.

Diamond, Jared. *Guns, Germs and Steel: The Fates of Human Societies*. New York: W. W. Norton and Company, 1997.

Engle, Dawn and Ivan Suvanjieff. *2012: The True Mayan Prophecy.* Film producer Ivan Suvanjieff, 2012.

Freidel, David and Linda Schele and Joy Parker. *Maya Cosmos, Three Thousand Years on the Shaman's Path.* New York: William Morrow and Company, 1990.

Gill, Richardson. *The Great Maya Droughts: Water, Life and Death.* Albuquerque: University of New Mexico Press, 2001.

Jenkins, John Major. *Maya Cosmogenesis 2012.* Santa Fe: Bear & Company, 1998.

LeBrun, David. *Breaking the Maya Code.* Nightfire Films, 2008.

Markham, Roberta H. and Peter T. Markham. *The Flayed God: The Mythology of Mesoamerica.* San Francisco: Harper, 1992.

Morley, Sylvanus G. *The Ancient Maya, Third Edition.* Rev: George W. Brainerd. Stanford, Calif: Stanford University Press, 1956.

Pererra, Victor and Robert D. Bruce. *The Last Lords of Palenque: The Lacandon Mayas of the Mexican Rain Forest.* Berkeley and Los Angeles: University of California Press, 1982.

Pinchbeck, Daniel. *2012: The Return of Quetzalcoatl.* New York: Jeremy P. Tarcher/Penguin, 2006.

Recer, Paul. "Study Links Demise of Mayan Civilization to Ancient Dry Spells." *The Associated Press* (March 2003).

Restall, Matthew and Amara Solani. *2012 and the End of the World.* Plymouth, UK: Rowman & Littlefield, 2011.

Schele, Linda and David Freidel. *A Forest of Kings, The Untold Story of the Ancient Maya.* New York: William Morrow and Company, 1992.

Sejourné, Laurette. *Burning Water: Thought and Religion in Ancient Mexico.* New York: Thames and Hudson, 1978.

Stephens, John Lloyd. *Incidents of Travel in Central America, Chiapas and Yucatan.*
Cambridge: Cambridge University Press, 1841, 2010.

Stuart, David. *The Order of Days: The Maya World and the Truth About 2012.* New York: Harmony Books, 2011.

Stuart, George E. and Gene S. Stuart. *The Mysterious Maya.* National Geographic Society, 1977.

Tedlock, Barbara. *Time and the Highland Maya, Revised Edition.* Albuquerque: University of New Mexico Press, 1997.

Tedlock, Dennis. *Popol Vuh: The Definitive Edition of the Mayan Book of the Dawn of Life and the Glories of Gods and Kings.* New York: Touchstone, 1985.

Waters, Frank. *Mexico Mystique: The Coming Sixth World of Consciousness.* Athens, Ohio: Ohio University Press, 1989.

Webster, David. *The Fall of the Ancient Maya: Solving the Mystery of the Maya Collapse.* New York, Thames and Hudson, 2002.

About the Author

Jeanine Kitchel's ongoing love of Mexico led her to the Yucatan in 1983, and slightly more than a decade later, she left San Francisco for a relaxed lifestyle in Puerto Morelos, a fishing village on the Quintana Roo coast, that she called home for 15 years.

Kitchel writes about Mexico, the Maya and the Yucatan. Her Tales from the Yucatan series can be found on planeta.com. She's written for The Miami Herald/Cancun edition, El Universal/Mexico City, The Herald/Mexico City, The News/Mexico City, The Baja Times, The Mexico Files, Sac-Be and Fodor's Travel Guide: Cancun/Riviera Maya. She has contributed to websites mexicopremiere.com, belize.com, escapeartist.com, sacbe.com, mexicocultureandcuisine.com, mexico-insights.com, knowmexico.com, and yucatanliving.com.

Her first book, a travel memoir, **Where the Sky is Born: Living in the Land of the Maya**, is available for Kindle on Amazon.com and on iTunes.

Kitchel writes a blog, Maya Musings (jeaninekitchel.blogspot.com/), and can be contacted through her website: www.jeaninekitchel.com.